PIANO TIME PIECES
Book 1

27 companion pieces to Piano Time 1

new edition

Pauline Hall

MUSIC DEPARTMENT

OXFORD
UNIVERSITY PRESS

OXFORD
UNIVERSITY PRESS

Great Clarendon Street, Oxford OX2 6DP, England
198 Madison Avenue, New York, NY10016, USA

Oxford University Press is a department of the University of Oxford.
It furthers the University's aim of excellence in research, scholarship,
and education by publishing worldwide

Oxford is a registered trade mark of Oxford University Press
in the UK and in certain other countries

ISBN   978-0-19-372785-4

Music and text origination by
Barnes Music Engraving Ltd., East Sussex
Printed in Great Britain on acid-free paper by
Halstan & Co. Ltd., Amersham, Bucks.

Copyright acknowledgement

Morning has broken (p. 5): text by Eleanor Farjeon. Reproduced by permission of
David Higham Associates Ltd, 5–8 Lower John Street, London, W1F 9HA.

Contents

Trick mirrors

David Blackwell

Lively

Spooks

Pauline Hall

Mysteriously

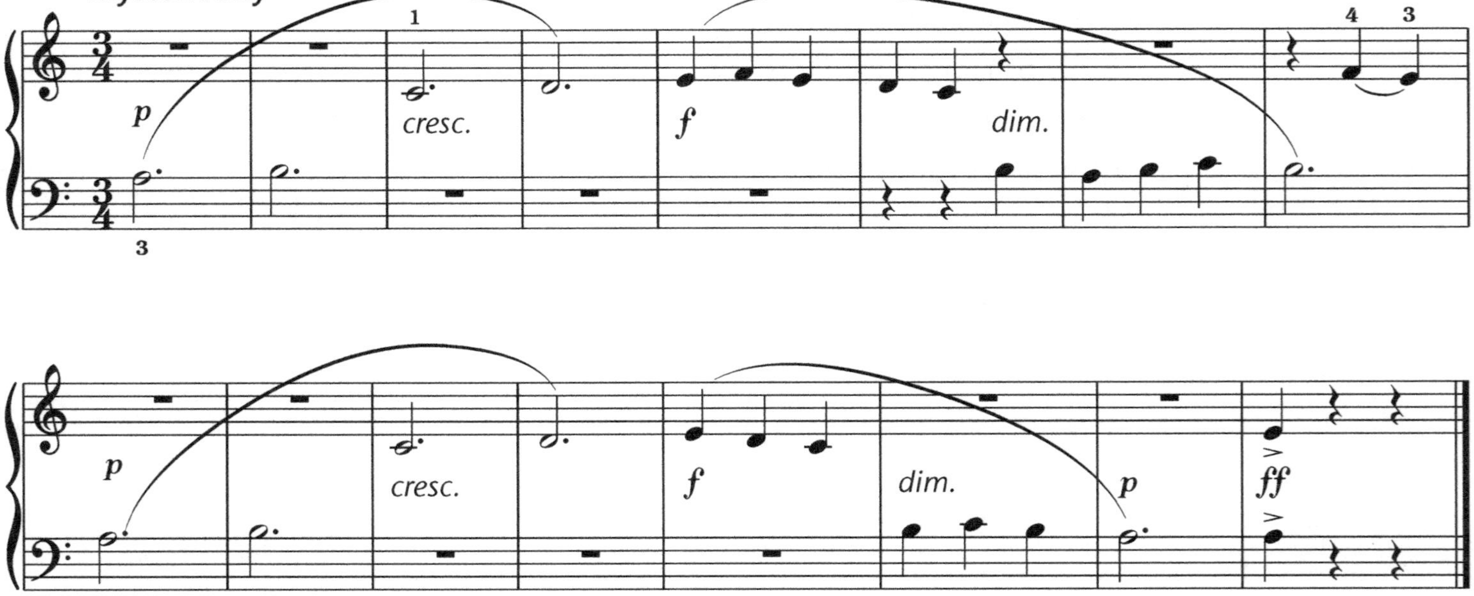

Morning has broken

Old Gaelic melody
Words by Eleanor Farjeon

Flowing
mf

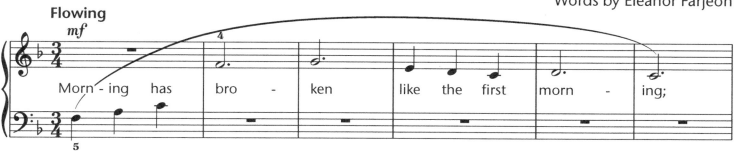

Morn - ing has bro - ken like the first morn - ing;

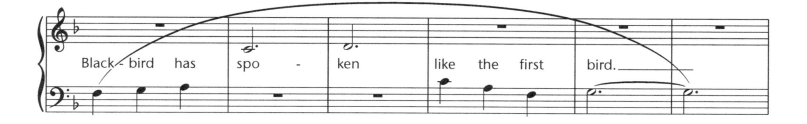

Black - bird has spo - ken like the first bird.

Praise for the sing - ing! Praise for the morn - ing!

Praise for them spring - ing, fresh from the Word!

Text reprinted by permission of David Higham Associates Ltd.

5

Grass so green

Czech folk-tune
arr. Pauline Hall

Very smoothly

Frog count

Pauline Hall

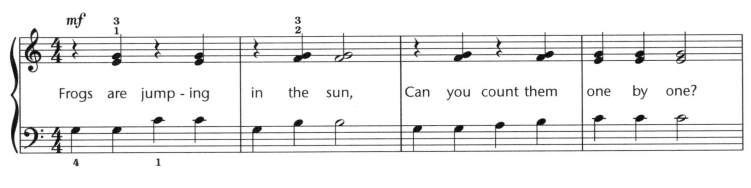

Frogs are jump-ing | in the sun, | Can you count them | one by one?

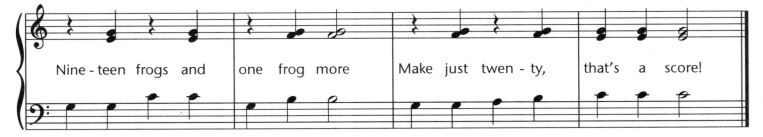

Nine-teen frogs and | one frog more | Make just twen-ty, | that's a score!

Allegretto

Daniel Gottlob Türk
(1756–1813)

Bohemian dance

Czech folk-tune
arr. Pauline Hall

Martians' march

Pauline Hall

Boldly

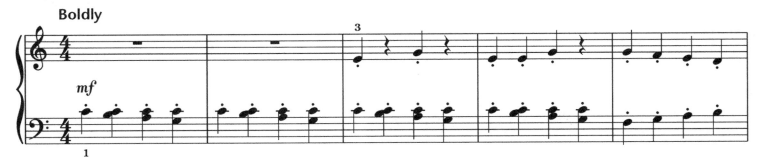

Crash land onto a group of low
notes as loudly as possible!

In the desert

Pauline Hall

Steadily

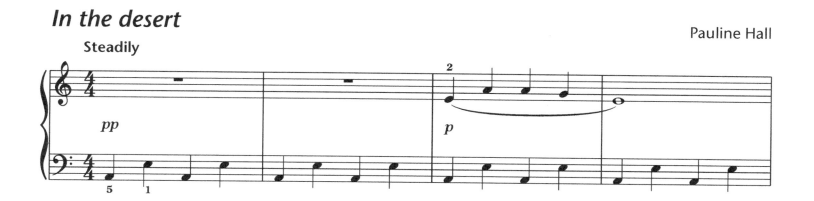

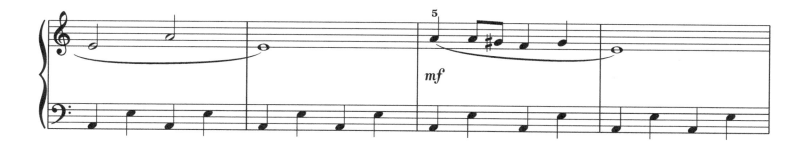

A chat between friends

Alan Bullard

Turpin

Pauline Hall

Tur - pin was a high - way - man, Tur - pin was a thief,

Tur - pin held the coach-es up on Houns - low Heath. He rode to Lin - coln,

he rode to York, He rode on Black Bess un - til he was caught.

The polar bear

Melody 19th century
arr. Pauline Hall

We sing of the po - lar bear, fear - less and bold; He

ne - ver feels hot and he ne - ver feels cold, Be -

-cause where he lives sum - mer ne - ver oc - curs, And the

rest of the year he wears plen - ty of furs.

On the river

Alan Bullard

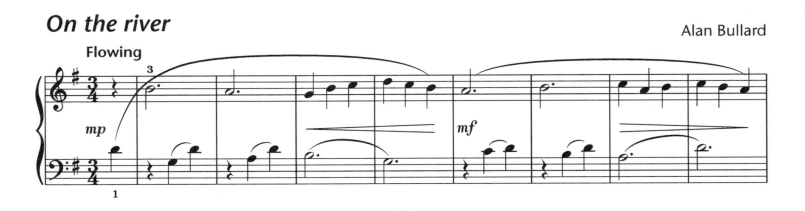

See what I told you—so there!

Pauline Hall

12

Chinese take-away

Here's a chance to invent your own tune!
Play steady F♯ and C♯ crotchets in the left hand. In the right hand, follow the rhythm given and make up a tune using the black keys only. The last note should be an F♯.

Steadily

Brave knight

Moritz Vogel
(1846–1922)

Like a march

Cheerful cha-cha-cha

Pauline Hall

Scarborough Fair

English folk-tune

Sadly

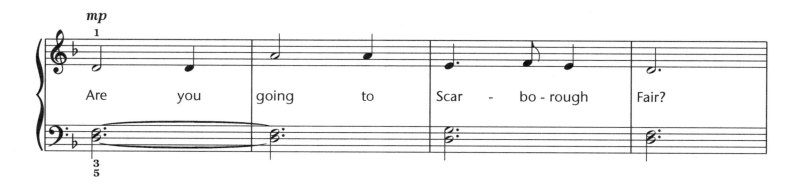

Are you going to Scar - bo - rough Fair?

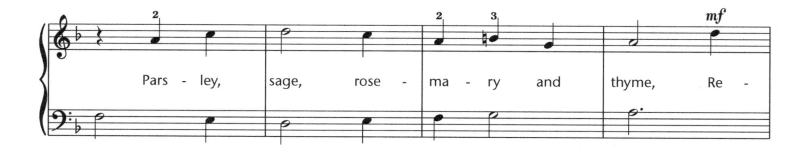

Pars - ley, sage, rose - ma - ry and thyme, Re -

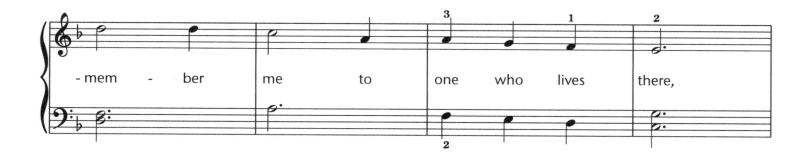

- mem - ber me to one who lives there,

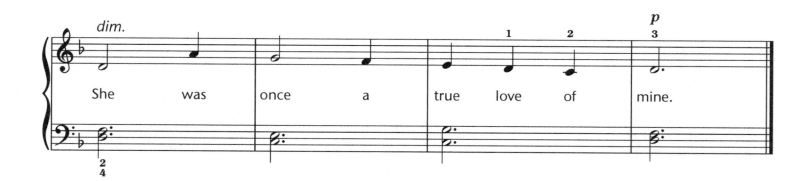

She was once a true love of mine.

Easy going

David Blackwell

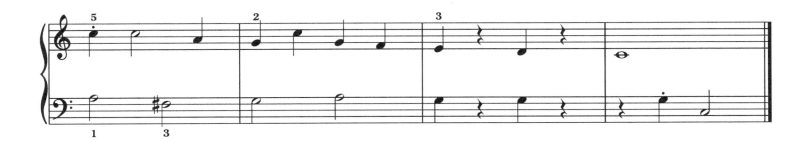

Polly wolly doodle

American traditional

The secret garden

Pauline Hall

You can use the sustaining (right) pedal to give a more mysterious effect. Put the pedal down at the beginning of each two-bar phrase, and lift it up on the last crotchet.

Slowly and mysteriously

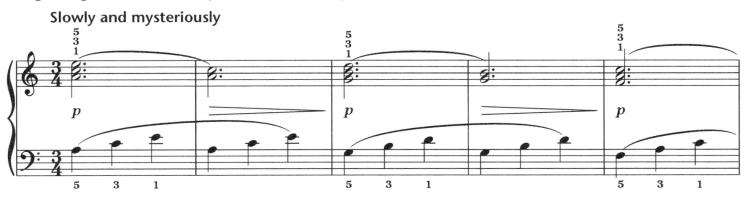

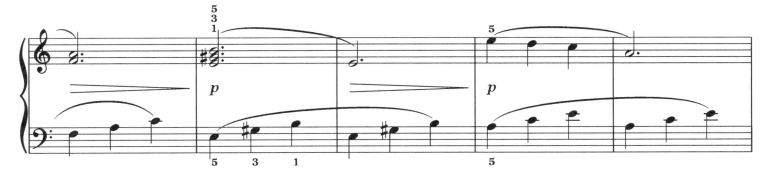

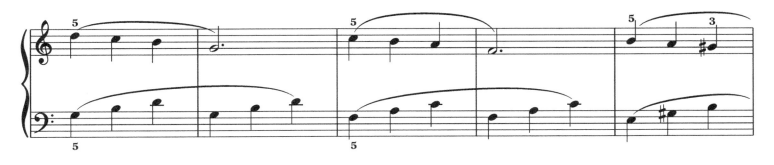

Michael, row the boat ashore

American folk-tune

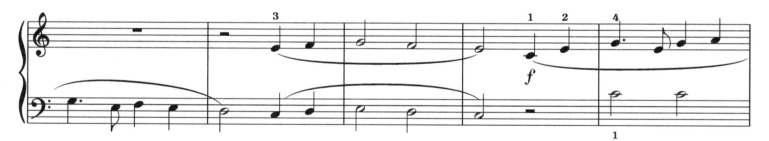

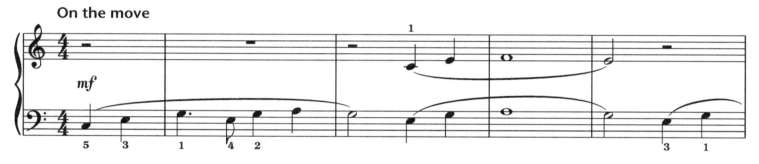

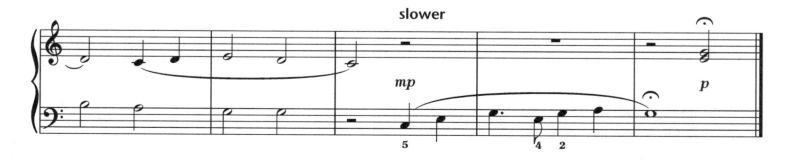

Crocodile waltz

Alan Bullard

Song of the squeaky door

Alan Bullard

The witch's lair

Pauline Hall

Wickedly

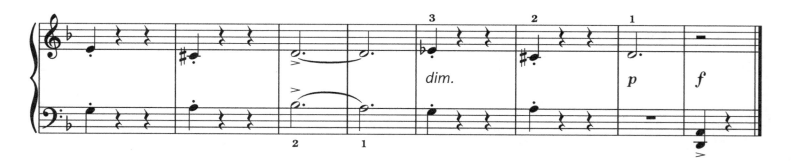

Two pieces:

Alexander Reinagle
(1756–1809)

1. Introduction

Allegretto

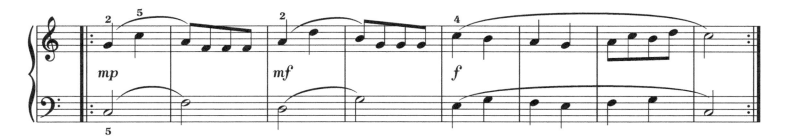

2. Promenade

Andante

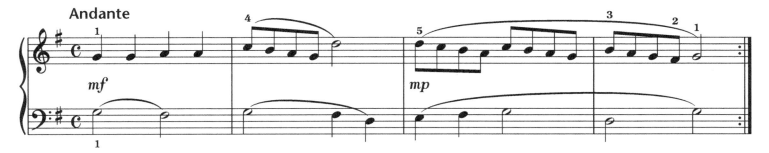

2nd time: **rall.**

Time to celebrate!

Alan Bullard

Rhythmically